hold her, but let her go

a collection of poems and notes
on healing and letting go

alysia quinn

hold her, but let her go © 2023 by Alysia Quinn

Rising Lotus Press
a division of Rising Lotus Co., LLC
Lakewood Ranch, FL 34202

For more, visit www.alysiaquinn.com
@alysiaquinnpoetry

ISBN: 979-8-218-29144-0

Library of Congress Control Number:
2023918550

Cover Design by Jayson Quinn

everything you've
been through
has brought you
right here.

and with the peeling
and shedding
of each delicate layer,
you are remembering
who you are.

for you & me

hold her,
but let her go—
the girl you used to be.

look her in the eyes.

embrace her.
forgive her.
thank her.
release her.

hold her,
but let her go.

Table of Contents

embrace her.

when i ask,
will you hold me?

i don't mean,
will you wrap your arms
around my body.

i mean,
will you be a safe place?
will you be the earth
to my bloom?

hold her, but let her go

like seeds and the sun,

and you.

so many things
of beauty
are hidden
before they rise.

i keep searching
for the part of me
that does not ache.

is she green or gray?
or forever blue?

a shade between
of infinite hues?

hold her, but let her go

in soft touches
in sunsets
in words of strangers

i'm still looking for you.

and all i see
is me.

i feel the weight
of the whole sky,

and i am in pieces,
scattered like stars.

what part of me
needed you
to be someone
you couldn't be

is where the work begins.

don't you dare
tell me to forgive.
i will no longer abandon myself.

instead, hold my hand.
give me my rightful space
to wallow in this grief,
to process the complexity.

tell me,
do you have the courage
to sit with me
in the uncomfortable
uncertainty
of it all?

hold her, but let her go

grief is looking
at how far back
i had to ignore the things
my heart was
trying to tell me.

most days,
i am more storm clouds
than sunbeams.

hold her, but let her go

this sorrow is like
a heavy, humid summer rain.

from seemingly nowhere,
amidst a sky full of sun.

i want to wake
each morning
without waging
the war of worthiness
before my feet
even hit the floor.

hold her, but let her go

the awareness of how
something about it
feels unsettling
in my body

is all i need to trust.

there are things
i cannot yet
put into words.

maybe i am
still softening
from cold seasons
of loss.

don't bother
with your half cups
of measured out love—
your just enough,
give some,
take some,
keep the peace
kind of love.

either love me
all the way,
or don't love me at all.

you had taken up
all the space
and every color.

i didn't even know
my favorite.

hold her, but let her go

you looked at my depth
as though it were a problem,

when the whole time
it was you who
wouldn't swim
my oceans.

go ahead,
sink me
to the bottom.

i learned
a long time ago
how to breathe underwater.

it terrified me
to acknowledge
that you used me,

and it still felt so good.

if you think
i am too much,

it is probably
because for you,
i am.

hold her, but let her go

remind me
how i am free
to get up from tables
with people
who never ask me
about the condition
of my heart.

if you wanted someone
so dear to you,
to choose you,
and they didn't,
i'm so sorry.

let me remind you,
you still have
breath in your lungs
and a fire in your soul.

you're gonna be okay.
you're gonna take this heartache
and turn it into something beautiful.
i know you will
because that is
who you are.

hold her, but let her go

when sadness descends,
i still have a hard time
believing it will ever leave.

the fog grows too thick
for me to remember,
i am a dark horse.

all of this feels
like the slowest death
and the most beautiful birth
all at the same time.

for some of us,
silence was
a survival tactic.

we learned early on
how speaking up to those
supposed to love us
meant receiving less love
or provoked harm.

so, if you're witnessing
the messy and courageous
transformational process
of someone finally
finding their voice,

you are witnessing a miracle.

let me assure you,
it is not a sign
of weakness.

this melancholy lives
deeply in your bones
because you were made
to hold heartache
a little closer.

you were made
to help show others
how to hold theirs, too.

despite all of the consuming pain
you felt in walking away,

the most beautiful thing happened
when you began
to discover yourself.

washed ashore by winds and waves,
weathered, wet, and salty—

i'm still standing.

more wild and bare.

more home to myself
and the birds.

hold her, but let her go

i am learning how

to take up

as much space

as i need.

it took me days
to look at what
you had written to me,
so beautiful and kind.

but if i'm honest,
it stings a bit.

i'm still figuring out
how to hold
all that goodness,
how to offer myself
that same love,

enough to slowly open
and allow it all
to seep into my flesh,
sweet and slow,
like honey.

hold her, but let her go

i can only know
and connect with you
to the extent
i am known
and connected
with myself.

give me storytelling, sad songs
with words that raise the hair on my arms
and linger in my chest.

give me dark, moody painted rooms
with light leaks and old books.

give me skin-tingly shivers
from his shoulders wrapping mine.

give me weathered, bare trees
and sunlit fields of flowering weeds,
the kind no one else wants.

give me the wild things in this life,
the ones that help me
remember who i am.

even if it turns out
those sweet times
with you were lies,

they were real to me.

so, this is where
i will hold you,
in these pages of poems
i fold into paper flowers,

the kind that never die.

i have never been good at following.
i have always wanted to find
my own way,
even if that means
being lost for a while.

hold her, but let her go

maybe, i just
see best
in the dark.

all of it left me
knowing how to
survive a storm.

it's living into
the ordinary
that i'm still learning
how to do.

hold her, but let her go

when you think
nothing is happening,
remember how the caterpillar
breaks down into softness
before she ever
gets her wings.

i am still discovering
what runs beneath
this skin—

perhaps, a wild current
i am no longer willing
to tame for anything
not meant to be mine.

i know there is so much
more evolving left to do
and many more layers to peel,

but today,
let me be enough.

forgive her.

here i am again,
reaching for
another beginning,
blinded.
fingers creeping walls
for the slightest crack of light.

shifting from the depths
of the dark night
into a burning shade
of the ripe,
orange morning.

no one else can
do this for you.

you must be the one—

to loudly,
and rebelliously,
and defiantly,
Love
what you feel
are the most unloveable
parts of yourself,
over and over again.

and this is hard.
and this is healing.

you are worthy
of yet another lift
out of this darkness.

you are worthy
of even more help
than you are
asking for.

some of us had to
break our own hearts
a few times
by going back
to situations
we just could not
reckon with.

and this too,
was part of the process
of learning
how to love yourself.

you were doing the best
you could at the time
with a really complicated situation.

you were doing the best
you could at the time
with a really complicated situation.

you were doing the best
you could at the time
with a really complicated situation.

there are types
of loss
we still don't
even whisper about.

when i decided
i could not carry
your wounds around
any longer

and acknowledged
i have deep wounds
of my own

and that my pain
is the pain
to which i shall tend
to which i shall bear

and that my story
is the story
i shall tell

—when healing could begin

free yourself
by releasing the idea
that you hold the power
to change what happened
back then—

that it somehow
could've turned out
any differently
than it did.

go easy on yourself
about the choices
you made
while you were
desperately
seeking peace.

i grieve most,

not for the love
that was there
and now missed,

but for the love
i longed for
and never was.

at some point,
she had to be brave enough
to burn bridges
between herself
and those who
repeatedly showed her
they did not deserve
access to her soul.

hold her, but let her go

you don't see me anymore.

because i grew tired
of having to
mend myself
back together
afterwards.

i don't know if i will ever
see your face again,
but i will set every word
i never said to you
free on the page.

hold her, but let her go

this will be a journey
i continue to walk out.

and i must grieve the fact
that the only version of you
i have ever known
cannot go with me
any longer.

the more i walk
this path of healing,
the more i realize
just how much courage
is necessary—

to step into
those spaces
of uncertainty
and unease—

that i may be seen.
that i may be known.

when you finally left,
you felt so hurt and angry,
but they didn't come after you,
not to work things out or apologize.

and it nearly broke you.

i know it doesn't take
away the pain,
but you can't take
that shame on
and here's why.

you disrupted something
within them,
wounds they aren't ready to face.

and you're not in charge
of their healing.
you're only in charge
of your own.

sometimes,
letting go
is in a letter
never sent—

the truth
finally spoken
to no one
except yourself.

hold her, but let her go

there are people who stay
and people who leave.

either way,
let them.

i am still learning
to trust myself,
to come back
from the dark spaces i go
to feel it all,

remembering how things
will shift again,
how i have always
pressed my heels
into the dirt
and gotten back up,

how the breaking
always comes
before the rising.

perhaps all this pain
has been a gift,
carving canyons
in my soul,
weathered smooth
from the raging rivers
that have gushed from
my eyes,

allowing the light
to shine all the way down
into the dark valleys.

i think that over time,
we gained an unspoken
understanding of each other—

an understanding
that we would never
understand each other—

and there was something
so deeply sad,
and also
bizarrely, lovely about that.

hold her, but let her go

it wasn't all bad
is the hardest part
of letting you go.

i know it will
always be there,
but like feathers
upon shoulders
or cinder blocks
between blades,

the way i carry
this grief
is different
each day.

every time i pour
a jar of spaghetti sauce
into the pot,
i am 9 years old.

without fail,
i remember to add
a little sink water,
replace the lid,
swish it around,
emptying
every
last
drop.

i was taking notes
of your every move,
desperate for you
to teach me
what you knew about
how to be a woman.

no one told me—
not the other moms,
nor my own,
not the doctor,
or the church groups.

no one told me
that if i am
doing it right,

becoming a mother
would mean
a complete undoing
and rebuilding
of myself.

hold her, but let her go

each time i let you go,

    i am left tending
    to another layer
    in the landscape
    of my wilderness.

of all the promises
you make,
the ones you make
to yourself
matter most.

hold her, but let her go

i sometimes forget
that letting you go
is not something
i have already done.

it is something
i must practice
doing every day.

i am not sure
i will ever make peace
with it all.

what i can do
is make peace with
the part of my heart
that desired goodness.

hold her, but let her go

when you cannot find the words—

find your breath.
find your tears.
find your scream.

these wounds
will not be quiet.

they still weep
a song of hope.
for you.
for me.

the reason it hurts so much
is because the healing you've done
has allowed your heart to soften.

you've let some people in.
you've let yourself
feel again,
love again,
and that is both brave
and beautiful.

so much of this healing
is listening to what
it is i need

and then being willing
to give it to myself.

don't forget to remind yourself
how much courage
it has taken
for you to use
your voice,

even when it has quivered.

if being lost
is the prerequisite
to being found,

then take all the old versions
of myself
and leave them
where and with whom
i loved.
let me find them,
again and again.
let me tell them,
everything belongs.
and that everything is going
to be beautiful.

after all this time,
there are seemingly
no step by step instructions
or timelines
in the layers and complexities
of healing and letting go.

all i know so far,
is that seeking beauty
is the balm
and acceptance
is the path,

while this body waits
for the gift of safety
to reveal her secrets.

so, keep it slow.
kiss the wound.

thank her.

she knows how to soften,

how to fade tenderly,

as if all along
she always knew
she was
pink morning sky.

and then one morning,
you awake to see,
a few petals
have unfolded.

so much of this growth
takes place
in subtle shifts,
in the dark,
in the quiet.

i don't know your story,
but i know you've
been through it.

because something happens to us
after we've gone through
a time of significant darkness,
after we've died a little,
after we give grief its rightful name.

we begin listening to our bodies,
and the next thing we know,
we're noticing sunsets
and the way the trees sway
before a storm.

and we settle in, we soften.
we see people with stories,
not just circumstances.
we stand differently.
we view pain differently.
because we are alive
in a whole new way.

you don't always have to
land on your feet.

sometimes, it is just about
the soft landing.

the one you allow yourself
to fall back into
without any particular form.
the one where you can
surrender to stillness
and enough space
to hear what matters most—
the resiliency of your own
beating heart,

and the quiet, guiding
voice within
that is wise enough
to lead you to
whatever may be next.

it may not feel
like it right now,
but all this grief
is moving you
into the next version
of yourself.

we do not feel the motion
of the earth spinning,
and yet,
she is.

give yourself time.
those lonely mornings
will eventually fade
into shared ones,
over warm coffee
and pancakes.

you'll open yourself
back up to others
when you're ready.

maybe
what people want
to know mostly
about you

is that you intimately know
the ache of a broken heart
and the heaviness
of being human.

even with very different stories,
they want to know
if you have the capacity
to sit with them,
to see them
for all of who
they really are.

hold her, but let her go

we all have
darkness and light,
she said.

the question is,
how much of each
are we willing to see?

i have found myself
speaking your name again,

in tender memories
with tentacles
no longer strong enough
to strangle my soul.

it is
your
story to tell.

i would never be
who i am today
without you.

all that pain
brought forth
a garden
that needed
the rain to rise.

i hope you can look back
and see all the choices
you made to love yourself
when no one was showing you
how to do that—
when no one was watching—
when all things seemed to be
working against you—

when everything was breaking,
you were still fighting for something—
for you.

sometimes, loving someone
means letting them go.

and sometimes, letting them go
means loving yourself.

when you can't figure it out,
try coming back to yourself
however you do,
in a walk,
in the garden,
in a warm bath with tea.

all the best answers come
when we stop looking for them,
when we acknowledge they are
already within us,

trusting that they will appear
in the peaceful, quiet moments.

it is not always
about moving forward
to the next thing.

often times,
keep going
means coming back
to my breath.
to myself.

hold her, but let her go

even in the darkness,
i can still walk the path
by the light of the moon.

when i don't know
what you need
and you don't know either,
it's okay.

we can sit *together*
and figure it all out.

there is much beauty
in being met by others
who can see you,

all because
they've done
the same kind
of healing work.

never underestimate
the gift you are
in what you may feel
are your weakest moments.

your raw, messy,
vulnerable self
is what we all need.

grief is the wave
that comes for me—
a shape changer—
a relentless and
unstoppable force.

and i am learning
that despite
its disorienting nature,
it does not wish
to destroy me.

but rather,
it carries me
closer to home—
to the distant shoreline—
to the solid ground
on which i come
to stand—
embodying a deeper
understanding,
a deeper sense of love.

somehow, the love
i think i missed
still finds me
in the most
unexpected ways.

it remains to me
a very odd thing,

how all of that pain
can both cost
someone so dearly
and catapult someone
into their calling.

when you meet someone
who is wise,
understand that the wisdom
was not simply gifted
to them at birth.
it didn't come easy.
more than likely
that person lived
through darkness,
experienced great pain,
and came out on the other side—
a cycle of death and rebirth,
maybe more than once.

hold her, but let her go

i can settle in,
knowing,
there are things
about my life that are
still unfolding

and will be for a long time.

leave space

for someone to discover
something of truth
all on their own.

there is magic
in finding things out
for ourselves.

you and i
have already lived
many lives,
many stories.

we have each
been a few
different people,

which is why
it is so beautiful
to keep choosing
each other.

by now i believe,
no matter what story
we are living,
we will somehow
find each other
in this life
or the next.

after a while, i realized
that seeing the truth
and walking in the truth
are two different things—

one is brave
and the other,
formidable.

we find the tools
we need for healing
when we are ready.

have faith that they
will present themselves
and be open
to trying new things,
even if it feels
a little terrifying.

when we are hurting,
we naturally and rightfully
close our hearts
for protection.

and so healing
cannot be rushed,
nor should we shame ourselves
for whatever pace
we think it is
or is not happening.
the time we spend
avoiding our feelings
is part
of the process, too.

and so healing
is always about the
slow softening.
it is about feeling things, again.
and we do so when we are ready.

the truths we come
to sense in the shadows
cannot be sensed
in the light.

the darkness
is sacred space
for all things
created to rise.

may my imperfections
guide me to grace

and my practices
lead me to presence.

hold her, but let her go

all of this creating
is the gentle practice

of compassion
towards yourself

i hope i can let go
of what i think today
should look like
and breathe in
what it actually is—

remind me how it is
its own thing of beauty.

tell me how
one day i will look back
with longing as i do
the others,
realizing just how
precious it was.

hold her, but let her go

i wonder who
i might have become
without all these heavy
things i carry?

i wonder who
i am becoming
because of them?

release her.

i have been trying
for so long,
but i cannot
change the past
or make any
of what happened,
beautiful.

i can only try to make
the release of it all,
beautiful.

over and over,
like the letting go
of
a thousand butterflies.

hold her, but let her go

maybe it all
happened that way

to set you free.

one day, after the loss,
we ask ourselves,

who am i, now?

hold her, but let her go

listen and let your body lead,
into new spaces,
new rhythms,
and new rituals.

it's okay if things
are changing.
everything created,
expands.

art has felt
so very risky,

and yet it is
the very thing
you cannot keep
yourself from doing.

it is okay
to surrender
to the joy
that making art brings you.

the uncertainty scares you
and yet it is also
where all of the magic
takes place.

who is she?
who are you coming
to know yourself
to be?

discover her,
make space for her,

remembering that
you already are her
and she has been
waiting for you.

she was awakening
to the part of her
that had known all along
that only
the wild things
satisfy.

what if
you took it by storm
meant you met it
with softness?

like how the rain
soaks the earth
and then
everything blooms.

less rigidity,
more curiosity.

less boxes,
more keys.

it is not yours to try
and prove your worth
to anyone who cannot see it.

keep discovering and revealing
more of who you are each day.

the people meant for you
on this part of the journey
will appear.

what does the warrior do
when there is no more war?

does she sing with the birds
at the rise of the sun?
or seek a worn path
on which to go run?

does she dance underneath
the light of the moon?
or plant seeds in the dark
to tend 'til they bloom?

what does she do
with all this peace?

in the clouds casting
mountain shadows
and the shimmer
of light-kissed leaves

in the sway
of the wildflowers
and the eyes
of all the aspen trees

wherever i am,
there too
lies this grief.

we must lift our eyes
to see the sun rise.
and she will rise.
she will rise.
she will rise.

hold her, but let her go

i so easily forget
how much tending
and waiting
is required for the garden
that is growing
in my heart.

when it feels like you
will never come back to yourself,

make a bed
upon the fresh
blades of grass,
under the canopy
of green leaves.

remember that you are in
the circle of things.

your heart breaks
in a million little ways—

like all the days
that break
at dawn—

for the the light to enter,
it must.

stay close to those
who make space
for you to bloom.

run from those
who won't.

i left,
like the leaves.

with a silent goodbye.

it was the only way
i could let you go.

listen for the poems
spoken between
ordinary people
on ordinary days.

see if you can catch them,
like butterflies.

the universe will send you
guiding angels,
mirroring what you've
already spoken
as true,
about who you are
and what you are
here to do.

i took a walk today and found
a butterfly on my path.
she had lost the use of her wings.

nonetheless, she was perfect
and beautiful and made me smile.
i placed her carefully in my hands,
thanked her for letting me find her,
and told her i'd take her home to rest.

she whispered back,

i hope you'll write
a poem about me,
so that i may always
remind you,
how the beauty and joy
we bring to others
lives on past the end
of our days.

no one really knows
what you've been through
on the inside
to get to where
you are now,

but you do.

and you should be
so proud of yourself.

you are allowed
to change your mind.

everything changes,
like trees and tides,
seasons and storms.

finding myself
by writing poems
has perhaps been,
my greatest
act of rebellion.

she is
sunflowers and storms,
soil and soul.

hold her, but let her go

she is
song and sage,
sapphires and sorrows.

perhaps, the only home
i will ever need
really is right here,
always,

on the inside
of my own heart.

hold her, but let her go

if the trees
keep releasing,
keep rising,
keep reaching
for the light,

then so shall i.

my old life
was built
for someone
i no longer am.

hold her, but let her go

it is right here,
wander within.

the wound
is the door.

healing is walking through
your own door,
not carrying anyone else
but yourself.

it's choosing to embrace
your strengths and flaws,
while letting go of
the need for
anyone else's approval.

it's sitting with grief,
and mystery,
and uncomfortable truths,
while releasing everything
and everyone not for you.

it's deciding to
love yourself,

until you
genuinely
like yourself.

hold her, but let her go

you won't go back
to that place
the same way
you left it.

you left as a seed—

now a rose—
thorns and all.

remind me
how comfort
can be found
by seeking
all that awaits me
in the subtle beauty
of simple things.

hold her, but let her go

do not starve your soul.
feed it with everything you crave.

run
sing
devour

like the creature
of nature you are.

we must
prepare our hearts
for the extraordinary
by surrendering to curiosity,
expanding our imaginations,
and believing that we are
in fact
worthy of receiving.

it's okay for our ideas
about the kind of life
we desire to change
as we grow and learn
more about who we are
and what we need.

it's okay for new dreams
to replace the old dreams.

resistance rests
sword in hand
on my chest.

and now i know
i am moving towards
the edge
of something new.

the road is long
from surviving to dreaming.

to be here now,
in this place,
is to begin to imagine
all of this differently.

i have the life
i once prayed for

and now i know
i deserve
so much more.

hold her, but let her go

the most beautiful
thing about you
is the way
you are rewriting
your story.

i will not lay to rest
without living this life
to the fullest.
i will not leave this earth
with my song
still left to be sung
or my words caged up
in my chest.
because i will be brave enough
to say them,
even if no one is listening.

i will teach myself,
no matter how long it takes,
to choose curiosity and love
over fear,
over and over again.
and i will learn how to love
more and more, and better.
because
i am on the journey of remembering
who i am.
and who i am is Love.

hold her, but let her go

sing from your soul
over every holy place of death
in your story.
serenade the dry, cracked pieces
and let them rise
into a new kind
of wild beauty.

one day, you won't need
to grasp so tightly
to a story squeezed to death
through your fingers.

you will gently
open your palms,
cradling those past chapters
in one hand,
and reaching for
what is next
with the other.

hold her, but let her go

do the birds know
they are free?

how do we know
when we are?

hold her,
but let her go—
the girl you used to be.

look her in the eyes.

embrace her.
forgive her.
thank her.
release her.

hold her,
but let her go.

you are more than
the things you have survived.
you are more than
all of your pain.

you are a slow
and meticulously formed
beauty.

Alysia Quinn is a poet whose writing speaks of healing, grief, trauma, and the path of self-discovery. It is her mission to share her authentic voice and story through creative writing. She hopes that her work offers a source of encouragement, strength, meaning, and beauty to those walking a healing path.

for more, visit www.alysiaquinn.com
@alysiaquinnpoetry